PIRATES, SWASHBUCKLERS AND BUCCANEERS OF London

First published in 2003 by Watling St Publishing
The Glen
Southrop
Lechlade
Gloucestershire
GL7 3NY

Printed in Italy

ISBN 1-904153-17-8

24681097531

Design: Maya Currell
Cover design and illustration: Mark Davis
Cartoons: Martin Angel

PIRATES, SWASHBUCKLERS AND BUCCANEERS OF London

Helen Smith

WATLING STREET

This book is for Charlie, Lucy, Harry and Joe.

Contents

A Pirate's Life For Me

Imagine you find a way to travel back in time, and you decide to sneak into a dark room in a tavern in Wapping, about three hundred years ago, when the Thames was full of ships and the taverns were full of sunburned pirates home on shore leave, laughing and drinking and swapping stories about their adventures.

It's evening time when you get there. You stand outside in the dark for a little while, trying to gather up all your reserves of courage. You pull your jacket around you, put your head down and weave your way in between the people in the busy tavern to make your way into the back room. The stink hits you immediately – a sweaty, salty, tarry, beery smell. You breathe through your mouth and go inside anyway – you want to hear what they're saying, don't you?

A pirate crew is sitting huddled around the fire, shivering a little bit in the unfamiliar cold. One of them grumbles about how much he's missing the Caribbean sunshine.

The pirates are fit and strong and mean-looking, heavily armed with knives and guns. Some of them have tied back their long hair with scarves, others have coated their hair in tar and fashioned it into a ponytail. They have gold chains around their necks and gold rings in their ears. One of the pirates has chunky gold rings set with rubies and emeralds on his thick, stubby fingers. The rings look a bit odd because his hands are covered in scars and tar from handling the ropes on their ship.

Would you be fascinated or repelled by the pirates? Maybe you're not sure yet. Maybe you need to know a bit more about their lives?

If you creep further inside and hide yourself in a dark corner of the room – pressing yourself against the wall and standing very still so the light from the fire doesn't illuminate your face and give you away – you might be able to hear them talking.

You'd have had to concentrate very hard to understand what the pirates were saying because they'd be using a mixture of sailors' slang and foreign words they'd picked up abroad. Listen ... there's something else that's very odd: now and again, an angry-sounding foreign voice interrupts the talk, repeating the same phrase over and over again, as if it's very important. You strain to hear the phrase, trying to understand what's being said. You hear the phrase over and over – is it something about treasure? You wait impatiently for your eyes and ears to adjust to your surroundings.

You lean forward a little – not too much, in case you are discovered – and realize the angry-sounding voice is not coming from a small, angry foreign man. It's coming from a parrot that one of the pirates has brought home to be sold in the tavern – later on, the landlord will advertise it in a newspaper for sale to the public as a magical talking bird.

As you stand in the tavern, you hear tales of desert islands, of exotic food and of battles fought and won against other pirates. The pirates are getting a little bit drunk now, clanking their tankards together as they toast each other and call for more ale. A pirate's life is very free and easy, they agree. It's the only way to live – with all decisions put to a vote and all treasure shared.

You listen to them repeating the legends of pirate captains who are supposed to have buried their treasure on deserted islands or brought it back to London and hidden it in tavern cellars. Maybe there is some hidden here, under the stone floor underneath your feet? The pirates say they'd love to get their hands on that treasure. Well, who wouldn't?

As the evening draws to a close, the pirates use small, roughly shaped foreign gold coins to pay for ale and then they stagger upstairs to their lodgings. It's time for you to leave, too, and come back to the twenty-first century.

But maybe, instead of going home, you're tempted to go up to the pirates and ask if they could take you with them as a cabin boy to learn the ropes (even if you're a girl, it doesn't matter; keep your hair short and dress up as a boy. Lots of girls have done it and hardly anyone seemed to notice). Maybe you think they'll take a look at you and laugh, pinching and poking at you, saying you're too puny to fight, why should they take you on board and give you a share of their treasure? In that case, you could find out the name of their ship and stow away on board instead, hiding behind big coils of ropes or pens full of pigs or sheep or other animals, waiting until the ship's too far out to sea to turn back before you reveal yourself.

Would you be tempted? Plenty of young Londoners were – in fact, most of the young men who joined pirate crews originally came from London. But maybe you'd better find out a bit more before you make your decision ...

CHAPTER ONE

Fame, Fortune and ... Death

What do you want to do when you grow up?

I bet people ask you all the time what you want to do when you grow up. Uncles and aunties and friends of your parents are the worst but sooner or later everyone asks, don't they? And when you don't answer them, they start making suggestions – policeman, actress, doctor, teacher ...

Has anyone ever suggested a career as a pirate captain?

Why not try this three-point checklist to see whether it would suit you?

1. Looking for fame?   Yes ✓
Pirate captains made reputations so fierce that we still know their stories today, hundreds of years later. Have you heard of Francis Drake, Captain Morgan or Blackbeard? They were all pirates.

2. Looking for a fortune?   Yes ✓
Some pirates stole treasure that would be worth millions of pounds in today's money.

3. Looking for death?   Ah, no, not really ...
Unfortunately most pirates had short, violent careers that usually lasted no more than three or four years. Some were killed in battle and some were captured, tried and executed at Wapping. There weren't very many who died of old age.

Oh well, two out of three isn't too bad.

Now, about that treasure ...

Treasure

Before aircraft were invented, the only way to get supplies from overseas to England was to bring them in by ship.

Ships didn't just carry gold and jewels – here are some of the 'treasures' that pirates took away with them when they raided other ships:

Old Rope

When pirates attacked and plundered other ships, they weren't always looking for gold. They often needed to get hold of food and drink, or sails, ropes and tools to repair their ships.

Sugar and Spice and All Things Nice

In the 1700s, 1800s and 1900s, merchant ships carried cargoes of spices, tobacco, rum, wine, oranges, pepper, silk, raisins, cotton and tea across the sea. London was by far the biggest port in England, with many English merchant ships coming in and out of London.

Lions and Tigers and Elephants and Bears

A few ships carried exotic animals caged in the hold – tigers, monkeys, giraffes, elephants and bears – to be exhibited or studied or presented as gifts to the kings, queens and emperors of Europe. Some of the animals ended up in the Royal Zoo at the Tower of London. Some of them didn't make it anywhere – they died at sea.

People

One shocking trade, legal in the British Empire until 1807, was the trade in people. Men and women were forced from their homes in Africa, chained together, transported across the sea in terrible conditions and – if they survived the journey – they were made to work as slaves.

All these cargoes, even the human ones, were targets for pirates. As trade increased between Europe and the 'New World' of America, the cargoes became more and more valuable, and piracy became more and more of a problem. There were so many pirates operating between 1700 and 1725 that these years became known as the Golden Age of Piracy.

This must have been a great time to be a pirate. But it wasn't such a great time if you were an ordinary ship's captain, or a merchant, trying to import goods into England.

So, something had to be done ...

The Royal Proclamation

King George 1 of England was living in the Golden Age of Piracy.

By 1717, King George 1 was very cross.

He'd HAD ENOUGH of Piracy!

On 5 September 1717, from his palace at Hampton Court, the king issued a Royal Proclamation to try to put an end to it.

He declared that any British Pirates operating in the West Indies would be pardoned if they gave themselves up before 5 January 1718.

If they didn't give themselves up, they would be hunted down by a specially appointed naval force.

The king offered a reward to every man aboard any ship that captured a pirate captain on or after 6 September 1718.

If you were a pirate in 1717, would you give yourself up?

CHAPTER TWO

Why Our Stories Begin and End at Wapping

Wapping Wharves, Docks and Taverns

The names of streets and places in Wapping today are reminders of its history. Go to Wapping and have a look around, or open an A-Z, and see if you can find these places and guess what happened there, hundreds of years ago:

- **Tobacco Dock**

- **Cinnamon Quay**

- **Gunwhale Close**

- **Cinnamon Street**

- **Ivory House**

- **Sugar Quay Walk**

- **Silvertown**

You can imagine porters unloading valuable cargoes (the ones that survived attacks by pirates, that is!). Tea, coffee, sugar, pepper, spices, wine, oranges, raisins, cotton, silk, tobacco, silver, gold, copper, tin and jewels were unloaded on the wharves and stored in the warehouses along the river, or taken by barge or by road to other parts of the country.

Hundreds of years ago, the River Thames was a crowded, busy, working waterway. Here are some of the things that would have been going on:

• Merchant ships loaded and unloaded their cargoes at the docks.

• Sailors from ships that had been moored at sea were collected, brought into London and ferried out again.

• Sailors' wives and girlfriends were taken to visit their husbands on board ship if the men couldn't come ashore.

• Medium-sized boats and ferries went up and down the river carrying passengers and goods.

• Small boats carried fishermen who earned their living fishing in the Thames, and men with the nastier job of trawling for dead bodies and rubbish.

• Kings and queens travelled on the Thames in magnificent royal barges, decorated in gold and rowed by up to twenty men.

• Watermen made a few pennies rowing people across from one bank to another because, for hundreds of years, London Bridge was the only bridge that spanned the Thames. And even that kept burning down!

Pretty much everyone who lived near the Thames was involved with the sea or the river in some way. They weren't only sailors – there were also dockers, porters, laundrywomen, seamstresses or keepers of the taverns that served the thirsty sailors and gave them a bed for the night when they came ashore.

The Wapping Taverns

The taverns in Wapping just sold beer, right? Wrong!

The taverns were used as meeting places for sailors, pirates and press gangs (who signed up men for the navy, sometimes against their will).

You could also

• have your dinner there

• find a bed for the night

• rent a room if you were sick

• gamble

• buy and sell just about anything

FOR SALE!

Birds!
Parrots, parakeets and budgerigars were offered for sale in London taverns in the 1700s. Sailors bought them abroad cheaply and sold them to the landlords.

Flowers!
In 1780 a sailor arrived in Wapping with a plant that had never been seen in England before. The plant had exotic purple and pink flowers like a sultan's turban. The story varies but either he sold it in a local tavern called the Prospect of Whitby for a pint of rum or he gave it to his mother, who planted it in her window box. (Which story do you believe?) Either way, the plant was bought by a gardener and became known as the fuchsia (pronounced few-sha).

Sailors

Wapping tavern keepers were not celebrated for their honesty. Many of them were 'crimps' who tricked sailors into joining a ship and then took a reward of around 10 guineas each for them. The landlords kept boxes of clothes to disguise sailors who wanted to desert from their ships. They took in and cared for sick sailors and then encouraged them to get into debt with drinking or gambling as they were recovering, so the sailors had no choice but to sign on with a privateer to get an advance on his wages to repay the landlord.

Every day men and boys left London sailing down the Thames on merchant ships, on slaving ships, on warships operated by privateers, or on naval vessels. Some made their name as explorers. Others made their fortune as adventurers. Some returned to be tried as pirates and hanged at Execution Dock in Wapping, at the bend of the river between Wapping New Stairs and King Edward's Stairs.

You can still visit the site of Execution Dock today, and at low tide you can see the posts used to chain the pirates while their bodies were left to 'drown' in three tides as a warning to others.

Execution at Wapping

There was quite a ritual involved.

A pirate would be tried in front of a judge at the Admiralty and, if convicted, he would be brought in a cart in a procession from Marshalsea Prison along the Thames towards Execution Dock at Wapping. (All pirates were executed here until the Golden Age of Piracy, when there were so many pirates to be executed that they changed the law so that they could be executed abroad as well). The Admiralty marshal rode a horse and carried a silver oar in front of the procession.

There was time for the pirate to have a last drink of ale at the Turk's Head tavern before reaching the scaffold. Then, in front of a crowd of people watching from barges and ships on the Thames as well as from the shore, the pirate would be 'turned off' – dropped from the scaffold so that the rope choked him. Pirates were expected to wear their finest clothes and to give a brave speech before they died. It was considered very important for a man to die bravely. Once they were dead, the pirates' bodies were chained up at the low water mark and three tides were allowed to wash over them, symbolizing a shameful death by drowning. After that, their bodies were covered in tar to stop them from rotting, then put in a man-shaped iron cage (these were specially measured before the execution) and exhibited somewhere like Tilbury, Woolwich or the Isle of Dogs, where they could be seen by everyone aboard a ship going in or out of the Thames. Some, like Captain Kidd, were left there in cages for as long as two years, to remind others what their fate would be if they became pirates. The last men to be hanged at Execution Dock were George Davis and William Watts, who were hanged for murder and mutiny on the high seas on 17 December in 1830. From the river Execution Dock is marked with a large letter 'E' on the building at the site of Swan Wharf. The Gallows were transferred here from St Katherine's Dock in Elizabethan times.

Captain Clinton and Captain Purser's Gold Lace and Buttons

Captain Clinton and Captain Purser were tried for piracy by Sir Julius Caesar (yes, really – he was named after the famous Roman general!). Sir Julius was a judge of the Admiralty Court in August 1583 and he sentenced Clinton and Purser to be executed. They dressed up in valuable gold lace and gold buttons which they distributed to friends in the crowd before they were hanged. Their bodies were left to be covered by two high tides.

Poor William Kidd – The Wizard of the Seas

Captain Kidd was a very unfortunate man. Nothing he did seemed to go right, even his own execution.

He wasn't even really a pirate, although he was sentenced to death for being one.

Captain William Kidd was a privateer and pirate-catcher who sailed in a ship called the *Adventure Galley* and was known as 'the Wizard of the Seas'. Unfortunately this wasn't a very appropriate title, as we shall see ... Captain Kidd had been given permission by King William III to attack foreign ships. This means he should have been safe from prosecution for piracy. But the poor old Wizard of the Seas didn't work much magic. His crew nearly mutinied because he wasn't very successful, which meant they weren't getting enough money to share between them. Captain Kidd accidentally killed one of his own crew by cracking him over the head with a bucket. He was kept for a year in Newgate Prison – almost unheard of in those days, when prison was used as a quick transit point before trial and execution. His long imprisonment ruined his health and deranged his mind. He was tried for piracy by six judges in

May 1701 (six! Usually it was only one or two) and sentenced to be executed for piracy.

It was obvious he was very drunk when he got to the scaffold at Wapping, which was a bit embarrassing. When the executioner pushed him off the scaffold, the rope around his neck broke. This was not supposed to happen! Captain Kidd fell into the mud, which was really embarrassing. He was hauled up out of the mud, a new rope was used and he was hanged all over again. Second time lucky. (Or unlucky?)

His body was left to 'drown' in three tides and then covered in tar and displayed in a cage at Tilbury Point for two years. This could have been humiliating but poor old William the Wizard was, naturally enough, past caring by then.

CHAPTER THREE

What Were Pirates Like?

What did a pirate look like?

A pirate could be any nationality, any race, any age. Most were men but some were women. Some even turned out to be women dressed up as men.

A typical pirate was:
- A man
- A Londoner (why were Londoners so desperate to go away to sea?)
- Twenty-seven years old
- Five foot seven and a half inches tall

An ordinary member of the crew might dress like this:
- A handkerchief knotted around his head or around his neck
- A knife
- Lots of stolen gold jewellery
- Bare feet

- A belt called a baldrick secured diagonally across his chest with a couple of pistols stuck into it
- Cropped trousers, sometimes smeared with tar to keep them waterproof

Sailing ships have a complicated system of ropes called the 'rigging' that allow the sails to be adjusted to make them go faster or slower. A pirate had to be able to walk or run around the deck of the ship without getting caught in the rigging. He wore cropped trousers so that they didn't flap around his ankles. A sword would have been too long to carry around, so pirates invented the cutlass, with a short, thick, curved blade – perfect for running through their enemies. Bare feet meant a pirate could easily climb the rigging to look out for ships. If he had long hair, a handkerchief tied around his head kept his hair out of the way. If he was bald, a handkerchief could protect his head or the back of his neck from the sun.

A pirate would keep a clean set of clothes in his sea chest, ready for when he went ashore:

- A blue and white checked shirt
- A red waistcoat with brass buttons
- Shoes with silver buckles
- White trousers
- A short blue coat

For special occasions (like a battle or his own execution) a captain would wear a flamboyant version of a gentleman's clothes of his time:

- A hat with a feather in it
- A wig, or his own hair worn long and curled luxuriously
- A cutlass
- Lots and lots of stolen gold jewellery
- A baldrick secured diagonally across his chest with up to six pistols stuck into it
- A shirt trimmed with lace
- Knee britches and silk stockings
- A fancy waistcoat, perhaps with gold buttons
- Leather boots

There was a famous pirate in the Caribbean in the 1700s called Black Bart who might have been better called Red Bart as he wore a red waistcoat, red breeches, a red feather in his hat, a diamond cross on a gold chain around his neck and four pistols hanging from a silk sash slung over one shoulder.

Here are some other distinguishing features of a pirate that you won't want to imitate:
- A pirate was usually tanned from working on deck in the sunshine.

• His hands would probably have cuts, scars and tar on them from pulling at ropes on deck.

• On board ship, a pirate would keep his balance by swaying from side to side as the ship moved with the waves. On shore, until he got used to being on dry land, he'd still be swaying as he walked, so he'd look drunk.

• OK, he probably was drunk. But there's not much fresh water to drink when you're at sea, so you have to make do with rum.

• He would have wounds and scars and bits and pieces of his body missing – an eye, perhaps, or an ear, maybe a thumb – from battles fought at sea.

• His teeth would be terrible. Pirates who didn't eat enough Vitamin C would get scurvy, which made their teeth fall out. All they had to do was drink a little bit of lime juice every day. They didn't know that until Captain Cook came back from a long voyage in 1758. Until then, the pirates tried to cure it with rum.

• He would stink. He'd have been wearing the same clothes day after day, night after night. Clean water was limited so washing was kept to a minimum. His beard would be stiff with sea spray and matted with food. He would have bad breath because of his rotting teeth. His mother wasn't around to tell him to wash his hands after going to the toilet, and anyway no one knew disease could be spread this way. He would smell of sweat, gunpowder, tar, and anything else he'd been touching – turtles, goats, monkeys, his bleeding victims...

• He would seem sophisticated compared to ordinary Londoners – using foreign phrases picked up on his travels and talking about territories that had only recently been discovered, six or nine months' sail away from London.

Pirate Rules

Pirates devised rules to stop themselves from falling out with each other, to ensure they were ready to attack and to keep their ships safe. Every pirate had to sign a copy of these rules when he joined up, to show that he was willing to share in the hard work as well as the rewards. Decisions on pirate ships were taken democratically – everyone on board got to vote on whether they agreed with a plan or not.

Remember Black Bart, the pirate in the Caribbean with the red feather in his hat? He was very fond of music, apparently. Here are his rules:

1) Everyone gets an equal share of the food rations.

2) Everyone gets an equal share of the prize – except the captain, who gets a double share.

3) No one to leave the company until everyone has earned £1,000 each. Anyone injured before this sum is reached will be compensated, depending on the injury.

4) No stealing from each other. Anyone caught stealing will be marooned on a desert island.

5) No gambling.

6) No fighting on board – quarrels to be settled on shore by a duel.

7) Keep your weapons clean and ready to be used.

8) No running away during battle. Cowards will be marooned.

9) No boys or women allowed on board.

10) Lights out at 8 o'clock – no candles below decks after this time.

11) Musicians to work every day except Sunday.

Here's the reasoning behind some of these rules:

Rules Nos 1 & 2 – Equal Shares

The concept of sharing equally was a very important part of pirate life. The pirates settled everything democratically, which means that everyone voted on the big decisions, like where to go, who to attack and even who should be captain. Don't forget, though, that some captains were vicious men. The pirates lived in the kind of democracy where they voted with a show of hands. It would have been a very brave man who voted against the captain too often – this is the reason why we have secret ballots in elections to choose the government. No one can see who you're voting for and try to intimidate you into changing your decision.

Rule No 5 – No Gambling

Gambling could lead to arguments – pirates were not very good losers – and so it was banned.

Rule No 9 – No Boys or Women

Boys as young as eleven were a common sight on naval and merchant ships, where they were trained as sailors. But they weren't welcome on pirate ships because they weren't strong enough to fight and so they couldn't earn a full share of the 'prize' – the treasure stolen from other ships. Women were banned in case they caused arguments between pirates trying to compete for their affections. Sailors traditionally believed that women brought bad luck if they were allowed on board ship.

Rule No 10 – No Candles Below Decks after Lights Out
The wooden ships had to be protected from their biggest danger – fire. A lot of gunpowder was kept on board and smoking wasn't allowed anywhere near where it was stored. The use of candles was restricted to be sure that drunken pirates didn't drop off to sleep with their candles still burning.

What rules would you devise, if you were a pirate captain? Is there anything missing from this list? Is there anything you wouldn't agree with?

A word about pirates and parrots

One story we should probably set straight is the idea of a pirate with a parrot on his shoulder. We know sailors kept parrots as pets or brought them back to London to sell in the taverns there. But a parrot on your shoulder? Think about it ... it would be very messy.

Pirate Currency

The pirates stole so many Spanish gold and silver coins that these were commonly accepted as pirate currency. No matter whether they were English or French, or where they were in Jamaica or Hispanola, it was Spanish coins that pirates were hiding in their sea chests and spending when they went ashore.

• The small gold coins they used were called *escudos*.

• The small silver coins were called *reales*.

• The *peso* was a silver coin, about the size of the £2 coin we use today. It was worth eight *reales*, or about £15 in today's money. *Pesos* were also known as 'pieces of eight'. They had the Spanish coat of arms on one side and on the other side the pillars of Hercules, with lines representing the 'new' and 'old' hemispheres of Europe and the Americas. This design was the basis for the dollar sign ($) still used throughout the world today.

• The *dubloon* was a gold coin worth eight escudos and was slightly bigger than the peso. It had the Spanish coat of arms on one side and a picture of the king of Spain's head on the other side.

Buried Treasure

Do you remember Captain Kidd? He was the pirate who was drunk at his own execution and who fell in the mud when the rope broke. When his treasure was seized, a list was made of everything he'd stolen. The weights are in imperial measures (the metric system wasn't used in England until much later):

1,111 ounces of gold (1 ounce = 25g)

2,353 ounces of silver

1 lb of jewels (1 lb = just under half a kilogram)

57 bags of sugar

41 bags of other stolen goods

TOTAL VALUE: £6,500

Everyone had assumed there would be treasure worth five times as much. The story went around in London that Captain Kidd must have buried the rest of it abroad on a desert island somewhere, even though there was no evidence that he had.

We know that Sir Francis Drake buried chests containing

gold and silver after the raid on Nombre de Dios – but he went back to retrieve them the next night. Maybe he missed one?

Blackbeard's crew said that the night before he died, he told them that no one except the Devil knew where his treasure was buried, not even his wife. This sounds like one of those stories that a pirate might tell in the taverns to make himself sound interesting. Or maybe the pirates were very cunning and had secretly kept Blackbeard's treasure for themselves. If they pretended he'd told them he'd buried it and no one knew where it was, then no one would come looking for a share of it, would they? Blackbeard was said to have fourteen wives, so perhaps the pirates were worried they'd all turn up at once and demand their share of the loot!

Even if pirates didn't usually bury their treasure, there's always a chance that treasure from a sunken ship was washed up on shore a long time ago and has never been discovered. Who knows, maybe as you are digging a sand castle on a beach one day, you will feel the edge of your spade tapping against something that feels more solid than sand but softer than a piece of rock. As you scrape away at the sand with your hands to investigate, you will see the top of a wooden chest, damp and slightly rotten, full of secrets that have been kept for three hundred years. The chest will be locked, of course, but the wood will be soft enough for you to to peel it away to reveal … What do you think? Rubies? Diamonds? Emeralds? Gold coins? Let's hope it wasn't full of bags of sugar, which were valuable in their day but which will have dissolved in two hundred thousand tides since they were buried.

What did you call me?

A pirate is the name for any thief or murderer operating at sea or on a river – anywhere that comes under the authority of the Admiralty. This even applied to people who sneaked out from the shore to steal from the ships in the Thames.

In 1634 William and Elizabeth Patrickson were hanged for piracy for murdering a man on board a boat moored in the Thames near London Bridge and stealing £100 from him.

Pirates, unlike privateers, didn't have wealthy backers to fund their expeditions and pay their wages. This meant they could keep their prizes for themselves but it also meant they would be poor and hungry between successful attacks on other ships.

There were all sorts of different names for pirates, according to where they operated:

Privateers attacked ships belonging to enemy countries and stole from them. But they didn't think of themselves as pirates because they carried a 'letter of marque' from the king or queen of their country authorizing them to attack foreign ships.

They could not be prosecuted for piracy in England so long as they carried the letter or marque and so long as they never stole anything belonging to an English ship.

Privateers were wealthy men or had wealthy backers – they had to put up a bond of £1,000 before being granted a letter of marque.

The 'prize' of the treasure or goods on board the ships they attacked was shared between the captain and crew and any backers who had funded the trip.

They were a useful addition to the navy in times of war, when they were asked to fight alongside the navy battleships. This arrangement suited the privateers who were patriotic men who were delighted to fight for their country.

Buccaneers: In the seventeenth century, Hispanolans who had been driven off their island by the Spanish banded together with Africans who had escaped slavery, and everyone else who hated the Spanish, and they attacked Spanish ships in the West Indies.

They travelled by sea but they fought on land.

They got the nickname *boucaniers* from the French word *boucaner* for the traditional method used in Hispanola of curing meat by smoking it on a barbecue. (The island of Hispanola is now divided and one half is known as Haiti and the other half is the Dominican Republic.) You still sometimes hear people call the French 'frogs' because they eat frogs legs, and the French call the English *les rosbifs* because they think we eat roast beef all the time. Americans have been calling the English 'limeys' since the Royal Navy started issuing a ration of lime juice to sailors to combat scurvy. So maybe it's not so strange the way the buccaneers got their name, although it isn't very romantic!

Corsairs operated in the Mediterranean and along the Barbary Coast (North Africa), which got its name because the Europeans called the Muslims of North Africa 'Barbarians'.

The Barbary Corsairs were Muslims.

The Maltese Corsairs were Christians backed by the Knights of St John.

The pirates of the Caribbean operated in the West Indies, along the coast known as the Spanish Main (Spanish-owned American mainland) and off the coast of West Africa.

CHAPTER FOUR

Pirate Ship Ahoy!

What did a pirate ship look like?

A pirate ship had to be fast and it had to look frightening, so that the captains of other ships would surrender immediately.

If you visit the replica of *The Golden Hinde* near London Bridge, you'll get an idea of what a pirate ship might have looked like. The pirates customized their ships, adding more cannons than other ships of the same size.

Pirates carried about ten times as many men so that they could easily overpower their victims when they went aboard. Speed was very important because the pirates had to be able to catch up with their victims at sea, and outrun naval warships that had been sent to hunt them down. The pirates removed storage space or even hacked away at built-up parts of the ship to reduce the drag against the wind and make it go faster.

We tend to use the word 'ship' to describe any large sea-going vessel. But there were all sorts of different kinds of sailing vessels, with specific names according to the number of masts they had and the way the sails were rigged. Technically, a ship had three masts with square sails on all three masts ('square-rigged').

Sailing vessels

• A **sloop** usually had one mast, although sloops used in the Caribbean could have as many as three masts. Sloops were popular with pirates because they were small, manoeuvrable and faster (at 11 knots) than most other vessels.

• A **schooner** usually had two masts but could have as many as five. Schooners operated well in shallow waters and were also capable of sailing at up to 11 knots.

• A **brigantine** had two square-rigged masts.

• A **frigate** was a small warship.

• A **cutter** had one mast with a square topsail.

• A **galleon** was a large, well-armed Spanish ship.

When they were carrying treasure, large fleets of them sailed together for protection against pirates.

• A **tea clipper** was a fast vessel (sailing at up to 18 knots) used to carry tea to London in the 1800s. The clippers took part in an annual race from the Canton River in China to the London Docks, with the first crew home getting a bonus.

• **Galleys** were oar-powered open vessels used by the Barbary Corsairs that were rowed by European slaves. This suited the corsairs very well because it meant they didn't have to rely on the wind to attack. It was very hard luck on the slaves. Captured at sea or even in raids on ports, they were kept naked and chained together, rowing the pirates around the Mediterranean until a ransom was paid for them or until they died, whichever was sooner.

The Jolly Roger

One of first things that would tell you there was a pirate ship ahead was the sight of the jolly roger, the terrifying pirate flag with its symbols of death. The jolly roger was a pirate flag. Each one looked

slightly different and it usually represented the pirate captain's special methods of terror. It was made of black silk, with red or white designs sewn on it.

A skull with two bones crossed under it was the universal symbol of death at sea – the picture was often sketched in the log book next to the name of a sailor who had died while on board ship.

The pirates used other symbols:

• an hour glass = time is running out

• a bleeding heart = death

• a sword, cutlass or pistol = death

• a skeleton = death

• red = blood = death

The message was clear – unless the captain of a ship was facing death. Captains often surrendered without a shot being fired, especially if he recognized the jolly roger as belonging to a particularly fierce pirate captain.

A red flag was used by pirates to show that they were

going to show no mercy ('give no quarter') unless the captain surrendered immediately. If you saw the red flag, the colour of blood, you knew that if you didn't surrender you were going to die unless you could get away fast enough, or unless you put up a good fight and killed the pirates first. If the captain surrendered, or even if he put up a fight and lost, a black flag showed that he could expect to be shown mercy ('given quarter') and his life and the lives of his crew would be spared. Of course, some captains surrendered and they were still tortured or murdered. That's the kind of thing that happens when you trust a pirate.

No one really knows where the name jolly roger came from, although people have made a few guesses:

Does it derive from 'Old Roger', a nickname for the devil in use at the time?

Or does it originally come from two French words for the red flag – *jolie* (pretty) and *rouge* (red)?

The pirates were very sly. Sometimes they didn't fly a red or black flag. They flew flags or pennants – 'colours' – to give the impression that they were merchant ships from other countries. Black Bart flew either the English ensign and the Dutch flag, so he could trick other ships into thinking he was an English or a Dutch merchant.

He had two jolly roger flags that he also used:

1. One showed him standing with a flaming sword in his hand, each foot standing on a skull – one representing a Barbadian, one a Martinican because the governors of Barbados and Martinique had tried to capture him and he'd vowed to punish anyone from those islands that he came across.

2. The other showed a skeleton next to Black Bart himself, holding an hourglass.

Blackbeard's flag showed the devil carrying a spear and an hourglass. Captain Ned Low's flag was black with a white skeleton plunging a dagger into a bleeding heart with one hand, and holding an hourglass in the other hand.

If you were designing a jolly roger for your own pirate ship, what would it look like?

CHAPTER FIVE

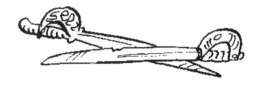

Life on Board a Pirate Ship

Would you enjoy life on board ship? Let's hope so – it's an important part of being a pirate! How would it feel to be running along in bare feet on the wooden boards of a deck warmed by the Caribbean sun? What about climbing ropes and looking out to sea for dolphins or treasure ships? It's not all like that, you know!

Do you like scrubbing barnacles off the bottom of ships? Do you like eating the same boring food every day? Do you like gambling and drinking rum? (I hope not!) Do you like sleeping in cramped conditions with everyone snoring around you? Are you not bothered about washing?

Maybe you get sea sick? You know that horrible feeling when you're on a boat and it's rocking too much? The colour drains out of your face and everyone tells you you've gone a grey-green colour. Your hands go cold and sweaty, you start feeling as if you're going to be ... urgh, out of the way, you think you're going to be ... bleurghhhh!

Here are some top tips for preventing sea sickness that have been given to me by sailors:

1. Eat something light, like a piece of toast, before you set off (no greasy food).

2. Get out on deck and breathe the fresh air, if you can.

3. Sit up straight, breathe slowly and evenly, keep your eyes on a fixed point.

4. While you are sitting down, take your feet a few centimetres off the floor (this doesn't work while you are standing, unless you are a magician!).

5. Sip ginger tea or nibble on a little piece of crystallized ginger. Ginger supposedly stops you feeling queasy.

6. Don't give in! Think positively. You can get through this.

And remember, if you do get sea sick, don't feel too bad. Lots of sailors get sea sick, especially when the weather is rough. They just get used to it.

Sharing the chores

Life on board ship could be hard work, but it could also be fun. Pirates were better off than ordinary sailors because pirate ships had more men on board than ordinary ships (so they could fight and overpower other ships more easily). This meant there were more of them around to share chores, like mending the sails and scrubbing the decks.

Every so often the ships had to put into shore and 'careen' the ship, which meant scraping the barnacles off the bottom of it, which was a horrible job.

Three reasons why the Caribbean was perfect for pirates to operate in:

1. There were so many deserted islands and private inlets where they could do the job – pirate ships weren't welcome in ordinary ports!

2. And while some pirates were scraping barnacles, others could be collecting fresh water or turtles' eggs or trying to catch wild pigs or just picking fruit from the trees.

3. If the island was inhabited, then they could trade with the islanders. The going rate was a dollar for a gallon of rum and fifty cents for twelve parrots.

Eating

Some ships had kitchens, known as galleys. The cook was often an old man who was too weak to fight any more, or someone who had been injured. After all, a one-legged, one-armed or one-eyed man could stir a stew of turtle meat and potatoes just as well as any other man.

Some ships didn't have room for a galley, and the pirates would cook by making a small fire on deck (as far away from the store of gunpowder as possible) and boil a pot over it to make their dinner. Of course, this worked best when the weather was good. When the weather was bad, or when supplies were short, the pirates had to fall back on eating hard tack. This doesn't sound very appetizing and it wasn't. Hard tack was a mixture of flour and water (no salt, no sugar) that was patted into square shapes and baked twice in an oven until it was very dry and hard. It lasted for a long time that way and so it was perfect for taking on long journeys. The pirates tried to make it taste a bit better by crumbling it up the way people crumble up rusks for babies, and mixing it with water or milk or (guess what? – only suitable for pirates) rum.

I'd give you the recipe for hard tack but it would taste horrible and you'd end up wasting some perfectly good flour

Here's a recipe for flapjacks instead. Have you ever had them? They're delicious. This recipe makes 15 pieces – enough for a small pirate crew. You can store them in a biscuit tin or a plastic sandwich box, they'll keep for a month.

Recipe for Flapjacks

75g margarine or butter
2 tablespoons of golden syrup
75g dark brown sugar (ordinary sugar will do, if you haven't got brown sugar)
150g porridge oats

1. Wash your hands and put on an apron.

2. Get an 18 cm square tin. Tear off a piece of the paper that the butter is wrapped in. Put a little blob of butter on it and wipe around the inside of the tin so that it's coated in the butter. If you're not using butter, use a piece of greaseproof paper and some margarine. If you haven't got greaseproof paper, use clean fingers to smear the butter or margarine on the tin.

3. Turn on the oven to 180 °C.

4. Put the margarine and syrup in a saucepan. Get an adult to turn on the heat on the stove for you and watch you as you melt the butter or margarine.

5. Turn off the heat. Take the saucepan off the stove and put it on a wooden board on a low table top in front of you. Stir in the sugar and the porridge oats, using a wooden spoon. Mix it up really well.

6. Put the mixture in the tin and put the tin in the oven.

7. Bake the flapjacks for 20 minutes.

8. Use oven gloves to take the tin out of the oven.

9. Leave the tin on a wooden board for five minutes to cool down. Leave it, I said! I know it smells delicious – go and do something else while you're waiting.

10. Cut the mixture into fifteen rectangular pieces – make two lines going one way down the tin and four lines going across.

11. Wait for the flapjacks to cool down.

12. Serve and eat.

Other long-lasting food that was brought along for the journey was salt pork and dried peas. Some ships also had hens (to lay eggs and to go into the pot for dinner, eventually) and goats (for milk and meat) and even sheep or cattle. The trouble with goats, sheep and cattle is that they need grass to eat, and grass is in short supply on a long sea journey. The animals would get scurvy and sea sickness, just like the men. And they couldn't be cured with rum. There were some other little creatures in the ship's stores that weren't so welcome. Weevils – little bugs – ate the flour and the hard tack. Rats ate everything. When they ran out of food the rats ate the floor boards and the ropes.

One thing about being a pirate is that when you ran out of food, you could just steal some more.

Entertainment

Musicians were a vital part of life at sea. They entertained the men below decks on long journeys. Everyone liked a sing-song.

There was often a mixture of nationalities on board a ship but if conversation was difficult (and after all, they must have got tired of teaching each other to swear in different languages) then it was quite easy to learn to sing a foreign song, especially with lots of repetition. If they didn't know the words, they could always la la la.

When they went into battle, the
musicians were there, urging them
forward. A fiddler might be high up
in the rigging, his feet twisted in
the ropes to stop him falling, his
fiddle under his chin, a red
handkerchief around his neck
to soak up the sweat and stop his
instrument from slipping, his right
arm furiously working his bow to play the tunes the men
would want to hear as they fought. And below him on deck, in
the middle of the fighting, a trumpeter sounding high, clear
notes that would frighten all the other ships around within
hearing distance. If there was a drummer boy on board –
more usual on a naval ship than a pirate ship – he would be
there on deck, steadily beating his drum, trying to keep his
nerve and do his job as the men fought and fell around him.
When they worked on deck, the pirates would sing rhyming
songs to keep their spirits up and to keep them hauling ropes
in time with each other. The songs were often rude and
colourful and were known as sea shanties (the word comes
from the French 'chanter', meaning 'to sing'.) Musicians
traditionally accompanied soldiers and ships into battle, so
it is not surprising that pirates liked to hear music when
they were attacking other ships. These days, if the old-

fashioned kind of pirates were still operating, do you think they would take a DJ and a huge set of speakers along with them? Would there be an MC with a microphone hanging from the rigging, shouting encouragement above the roar of the cannon as the pirates engaged in hand-to-hand combat on the deck below?

If you were a pirate, what tune would you ask the musicians to play as you went into battle and raided other ships?

Drinking rum

Apart from fighting, the pirates' favourite occupations were drinking and gambling. They weren't supposed to gamble on board (losing money to your friends soon causes arguments) but they did a lot of drinking.

Four facts about rum
1. It was the pirates' favourite drink.
2. It is made from molasses (treacle) and has a strong taste.
3. They drank it on its own, with hot water or mixed with fruit juices and spices to make a punch.
4. The pirate captains liked to have a (stolen) silver punch bowl in their cabin that could be filled with rum and passed round during celebrations and meetings.

Cats were kept to kill the rats. Dogs were kept to keep the pirates company. Monkeys, parrots and parakeets were kept so they could be sold in the taverns in London.

Sleeping and space

The pirates slept in hammocks and kept all their possessions stored in a sea chest below them.

* TOP SECRET! * KEEP OUT! * NO PEEKING! *

* NO BORROWING! * NO STEALING! *

The chest would contain:

• The pirate's treasure, including gold coins and jewels.

• A pair of clean white trousers and a short jacket for going ashore to impress the ladies, instead of the stinky clothes he wore all day, every day, and all night too, while he was on board ship.

• Tobacco that could be chewed (smoking wasn't allowed below decks in case of fire)

• Pair of dice or some playing cards

At night, after the candles had been extinguished to prevent fire on board, the pirate would lie in his hammock and try to get to sleep. It must have been difficult, with all the sounds around him – the wind rattling the rigging, rats scuttling and squeaking, cats pouncing on the rats, hens clucking, sheep baa-ing, the other pirates snoring, coughing and scratching or plotting in low voices, monkeys shrieking, parrots squawking, and the boards of the ship creaking as it bobbed up and down on the waves. The captain usually had a cabin of his own, with furniture, pictures, books, even a piano if there was enough room.

Going to the toilet and washing

The pirates would wee overboard into the sea – first making sure they knew which way the wind was blowing so they didn't splash their clothes! For anything more, they could go into the 'heads'. The heads were a couple of boards with a hole in them, mounted at the front of the ship, suspended above the sea. The fancier versions would be covered cubicles but privacy wasn't something to be relied on at sea.

Sailors on board modern ships still refer to the 'heads' even though they now have comfortable indoor flushing toilets with lockable doors.

If there was fresh water on board, it was used for drinking, not washing. The pirates had to wash with sea water. They would take a cup full of water from the communal supply and have a quick rinse around, keeping their clothes on (which explains why women on board ship could pass themselves off as men – they never took their clothes off, even to wash themselves).

CHAPTER SIX

Pirate Queens and Swashbuckling Women

Women weren't supposed to be allowed on board pirate ships. But if you were a woman and you were determined to be a pirate, you weren't going to let a little thing like that stop you, were you?

There are lots of stories of women joining ships as sailors. We only know about the ones who were caught or the ones who decided to sell their stories when they settled back on dry land. There must have been others who were never discovered.

Disguising yourself as a sailor was easier in earlier centuries than it would be now. Sailors worked and slept in one dirty set of loose-fitting clothes, washing hastily by candlelight from a barrel deep in the ship. There were plenty of boys and young men aboard ships who were still too young to shave, so it wouldn't have been strange that the women weren't growing whiskers. They would have had to be discreet about going to the toilet – no weeing over the side like the men – but they seemed to manage it.

The Curious Case of Hannah Snell

Hannah Snell was at one time the landlady of one of the thirty-six taverns in Wapping. She served as a soldier and a sailor between 1745 and 1750 until she was shot in the thigh. Although she managed to dig the musket balls out of the wound with her fingers, she was too badly injured to continue living aboard a ship. Hannah sold her story, published as *The Female Soldier*, and even performed at London's Sadler's Wells Theatre in military dress in 1750 to promote the book.

Women who were married to captains often joined their husbands aboard merchant and naval ships. Wealthy women also travelled as passengers. The women who went to sea disguised as sailors were often women or girls without much money who were trying to join their boyfriends abroad or on ship.

Penniless Ann Thornton and the Lord Mayor of London

In 1835, a penniless sixteen-year-old Irish girl called Ann Thornton was called in front of the Lord Mayor of London who had read about her adventures on board ship in the newspaper. Ann told him she had fallen in love with the captain of a ship at the age of thirteen and sailed from Donegal to New York as a cabin boy to try to find him, but discovered he had died shortly before she arrived. She tried to sail back from America to Ireland but her ship was diverted to the West Indies. Poor Ann then joined a ship heading for London as a cook but it was soon discovered that she was a girl. The captain said she worked as well as any of the men but she wasn't paid when she left the ship because she hadn't been a legitimate employee. The lord mayor felt so sorry for Ann that he gave her the money to get back to Donegal.

Privateer Mary Anne Talbot

In 1792, fourteen-year-old Mary Anne Talbot sailed to the West Indies dressed as a page boy so that she could be with her boyfriend, an army captain. When he was killed in battle, she joined a French privateer as a sailor, still only fifteen years old. By the time she was twenty-one, Mary Anne was back in London and her life story had been published. She claimed that she had been captured aboard an English ship in the English Channel and had been imprisoned by the French before heading for New York and then back again to London. As she wandered around the port in 1799, dressed in sailors' clothes, a press gang tried to get her to join a naval ship, at which point she told them she was a woman.

She appeared on stage at the theatre in Drury Lane in London, dressed as a sailor. She was imprisoned for debt before the rather fanciful account of her life was published in 1804 and she died at the age of thirty.

Charlotte Badger, the Pickpocket turned Pirate

Charlotte Badger was a pickpocket from London who had been transported to Australia. In 1806 Charlotte (described as very fat) and her friend Catherine Hagerty (described as very pretty), two boys and six men seized control of a brig called the Venus that was taking them to Tasmania, where Charlotte and Catherine had been sent to work as servants. Charlotte and the others sailed away to New Zealand, where she and Catherine set up home with two of the men from the Venus. Although she had only ever stolen one ship, Charlotte became celebrated as a pirate in Australia.

Anne Bonny and Mary Read, Pirates of the Caribbean

When they were children, Anne Bonny and Mary Read had both been dressed as boys – Anne in Ireland and Mary in London – so that their parents could swindle money out of family members.

Anne moved to America and married a man called James Bonny, who tried to make a living by supplying information about pirates. But Anne fell in love with the pirate captain John Rackham, known as Calico Jack, and ran off with him. Dressed as a man, she helped him steal a sloop and they began a short career as pirates, even though Calico Jack had accepted the king's pardon in 1718 and was trying to go straight. They sailed with a black flag with a white skull above two crossed white cutlasses.

Mary Read fought as a soldier with the army in Flanders, where she fell in love with a fellow soldier and married him. When he died soon afterwards, Mary disguised herself as a man again and joined a Dutch ship heading for the West Indies. When the ship was attacked, Mary turned to piracy and joined Calico Jack and his crew, including Ann Bonny. Mary confided in Ann that she too was a woman. Although they dressed as men when they were attacking other ships – wearing trousers and with handkerchiefs tied around their heads and carrying weapons – they liked to dress as women at other times.

In 1720 they were attacked by an English naval sloop near Jamaica. Anne and Mary fought very bravely – even turning on their own men, who were drunk and refusing to fight – but they were captured and tried for piracy.

They were tried and sentenced to death by the Governor of Jamaica in November 1720 and then both revealed they were pregnant and were spared. Mary Read died of a fever in prison in 1721. Calico Jack was hanged and his body displayed on Deadman's Cay, an island off Jamaica now called Rackham's Cay.

Queen Elizabeth I, The Pirate Queen

Queen Elizabeth I, born in 1533 and never married, was an enthusiastic supporter of pirates – so long as they were fighting on her side. She financed privateers with her own money and, as the sovereign, she distributed letters of marque which, as you know, were effectively pirates' licences. Elizabeth herself had been imprisoned in the Tower of London for three months in 1554 when her half-sister Mary was on the throne. Mary had been married to Philip II of Spain. When Elizabeth was crowned in 1558, at the age of twenty-five, she began a long and successful reign that lasted more than fifty years. During her reign as queen, in 1588, England defeated the Spanish Armada at a time when Spain was the greatest power in the world, with ten times as much money as England. Many of the privateers who had grown wealthy with support from the queen rallied to England's defence, including Sir Francis Drake, who was knighted for his role in the battle.

In 1580, Queen Elizabeth met Francis Drake at Richmond Palace to hear about his voyage and to share out the prize. He had stolen treasure worth about £500,000. He kept £10,000, his crew shared £8,000 between them. The queen and the other backers profited from the rest. Five tons of silver were put in the Tower of London. There was so much money coming in that Elizabeth extended the Royal Mint and had to build bigger storehouses at the Tower of London for the treasure to be kept.

The English Queen and the Famous Irish Pirate

Grainne O'Malley, a famous Irish pirate born not long before Queen Elizabeth I, in 1530, eventually offered to work for the queen in return for protection for her sons, after many years as an enemy of English ships. Married at fifteen, mother of three children, widowed and married again, Grainne had a fierce reputation as a pirate, commanding a fleet that attacked ships sailing between England, Ireland, Scotland and Europe. When her fourth child was born at sea, Grainne got up out of bed the very next day to fight off an attack by Turkish corsairs, a pistol in each hand. She killed the captain and hanged the crew. When one of her sons, Owen, was killed by Richard Bingham, the treacherous Governor of Connacht; Grainne gathered her allies and fought against Bingham and the English, using Scots mercenaries who were renowned for being ferocious. In 1592, when Grainne was more than sixty years old, she was finally defeated. Her fleet was seized by Bingham and Grainne fled to Ulster. She decided to write to Queen Elizabeth I to ask her to make sure her sons would not lose their land. In return, she offered to fight against the queen's enemies. Grainne followed up her letter with a personal visit to the queen at Greenwich Palace. Queen Elizabeth granted Grainne a small pension, freed her youngest son Tibbot and agreed that he and Grainne's other son, Murrough, should be protected. Tibbot took charge of Grainne's fleet and was knighted in 1603, the year that both his mother and the queen of England died.

CHAPTER SEVEN

Sir Francis Drake and The Privateers

Sir Francis Drake was a proud Englishman with a letter of marque from Elizabeth I that allowed him to raid enemy ships. He flew a flag with the cross of St George (and sometimes black pennants, to scare his victims). To the Spanish he was a pirate and they called him 'a master thief'.

You can visit a replica of Drake's ship *The Golden Hinde*, which is near London Bridge.

Francis Drake and the Treasure House of the World

In 1571, Francis Drake visited the port of Nombre de Dios in Panama, disguised as a Spanish merchant. He was there to spy on the storage and shipping operations for the gold and silver that the Spanish mined in Peru and Bolivia and sent back to Spain in treasure ships. Drake's efforts to keep his identity a secret were understandable; the Spanish would have been suspicious of an Englishman snooping around in what was known as the treasure house of the world. He looked around for quiet inlets where he would be able to moor his ship secretly and he tried to find local people who hated the Spanish and would be willing to help him. He met up with some Africans who had escaped enslavement by the Spanish and were living as outlaws in Panama. He realized they would be ready to take revenge on the Spanish who had taken them from their homes. In 1572 Francis brought his brother John with him to Nombre de Dios and together they attacked the Spanish treasure house, hoping to carry off enormous quantities of silver and gold. But they had just missed a fleet of treasure ships sailing for Spain so the treasure house was empty. Francis was injured in the attack and one of the musicians he had brought along – a trumpet player – was killed. Francis waited around for more treasure to arrive in Nombre de Dios, passing the time by making small raids on Spanish ships and stealing gold and silver from them. Eventually in 1573, with help from the Africans and a party of French privateers, Drake attacked a mule train with nearly 200 mules carrying 300 lb of silver each. He returned to England with around 15 tons of silver, to the delight of Queen Elizabeth and everyone

who had backed the expedition. The loot was worth around £20,000 in those days – many millions in today's money.

Francis Drake Loots and Plunders his way around the World

In 1577 Francis Drake became the first captain to take his ship (the *Pelican*, renamed *The Golden Hinde*) all the way around the world. Magellan's ship had been the first to circumnavigate the world but Magellan himself died on the journey. Even on this historic voyage, Drake was on the lookout for Spanish ships carrying gold and silver. He offered a reward of a gold chain to the first person to spot their prize and it was his own nephew who saw *Nuestra Señora de la Concepción* carrying treasure that would be worth around £12 million today. It took them nearly a week just to transfer the treasure to their own ship. When Drake got back to England, he visited Queen Elizabeth in Richmond Palace to tell her about all the treasure he'd stolen on his voyage, which was worth a total of about £70 million. Drake, the crew and his backers shared the prize. The queen, who had been one of Drake's backers, was naturally delighted. She had some of silver put in the Tower of London and then went to Deptford to knight him.

Francis Drake Singes the King of Spain's Beard

In 1587 Drake sailed into Cadiz harbour and sank twenty-four Spanish ships in what became known as 'the singeing of the King of Spain's beard'. Not surprisingly, Spain attacked

England the following year with an Armada of ships in 1588 but, with a mixture of luck and resourceful planning, including the use of fire ships, Spain's superior force was defeated.

Captain Martin Frobisher and the Fool's Gold

Captain Martin Frobisher set off to look for the north-west passage to China in 1576, sailing north over the top of Canada. Queen Elizabeth I, who was one of his backers, waved him off from a window in her palace at Greenwich as he sailed past on the Thames. Martin was a successful privateer who first went to sea when he was a boy. As a captain he had a reputation for controlling his crew by cutting off their hands if they got into a fight with each other. Martin discovered what he thought must be China but was in fact northern Canada. He landed and collected a sample of rock that appeared to be gold. Spain had its gold mines and silver mines in South America. England had nothing like this and wanted to find a source of great riches. In 1577 Martin went back again and this time returned to England with 200 tons of 'gold' and a man, woman and baby whom he took to be Chinese but who were in fact Inuits. They all died within a month of reaching England.

The Inuit man proved very popular before he died,

demonstrating his kayaking on the river in Bristol. The baby was brought to London to be presented to Queen Elizabeth but died and was buried in St Olave's church near the Tower of London, where Samuel Pepys is also buried. A gold rush started, with people falling over themselves to get involved in backing the next expedition to bring back more gold. The backers formed the 'Cathay Company'. (Cathay meaning China). And Martin Frobisher was called 'the Admiral of Cathay'. Unfortunately, tests showed it was not gold but pyrite – known as 'fool's gold'. However, one of Martin's backers found an alchemist who defied all the experts and did some 'tests' of his own that demonstrated that the rock really was gold. In 1578, still believing he had found gold, Martin assembled 15 ships and 400 men (many of them miners and one of them believed to have been a Spanish spy). He sailed for Canada in May and brought back more than 2,000 tons of the rock. The rock was put in the Tower of London and Bristol Castle for safekeeping but when everyone realized once and for all that it was pyrite, it was used to build walls and surface the roads. Frobisher redeemed himself by helping defeat the Spanish Armada in 1588 as part of Drake's fleet and he was knighted.

Unlucky Walter Raleigh

Walter Raleigh was a pirate and poet who was given a commission to explore America by Queen Elizabeth I.

She knighted him in 1585 when he outlined plans to establish a colony to be called Virginia after her – she was known as the Virgin Queen because she was unmarried. He is famous for spreading his cloak on the ground outside Greenwich Palace so the queen could walk over a puddle without getting her feet dirty. Walter was twenty years younger than the queen and obviously was only throwing his clothes on the ground and flattering Elizabeth so that she would take a fancy to him and make him rich and famous. This plan seemed to have worked for a while, although the Queen briefly had him thrown in the Tower of London when he got married without her permission.

When Queen Elizabeth I died in 1603, James I came to the throne and wanted to make peace with the Spanish. This meant there were no more excuses for privateers to attack the Spanish. Letters of marque were withdrawn and privateers who had made their living from attacking Spanish treasure ships found themselves on the wrong side of the law. Around half the people living in London's ports were sailors. With no wars to fight and no Spanish to attack, no doubt they wondered what to do with themselves. With no other income, many of them were drawn into piracy.

King James imprisoned Walter in the Tower of London for thirteen years for treason after accusing Walter of plotting against him. He was freed in 1616 and set off on an expedition to raid Guyana. On his return in 1618, he was beheaded for jeopardizing peace with the Spanish with his expedition to Guyana. His wife was given his head in a leather bag and she took it home with her to show her friends.

CHAPTER EIGHT

Sir Henry Morgan and the Buccaneers

Captain Morgan was a famous pirate who operated in the Caribbean. He was brought back to London in 1672 and he spent two years there telling about his daring exploits before being knighted by King Charles II and returning to Jamaica. He was supposed to be in trouble for attacking the Spanish but he was never punished. In fact, everyone was very impressed. There is even a famous brand of rum that is named after him.

The 'Admiral'

Captain Henry Morgan was born a gentleman in Wales in 1635 and became a successful buccaneer. He began his career as a soldier, ended it as assistant Governor of Jamaica and was happily married to his wife Mary for twenty years. He was appointed by Jamaica as the leader of the pirates, privateers and buccaneers operating in the Spanish Main and was given the unofficial title of 'Admiral of Brethren of the Coast' and authorized to attack Panama. An admiral is much more important than a captain! Unfortunately Jamaica had no authority to appoint Henry as admiral and shouldn't have attacked Panama as England was officially at peace with Spain. The Spanish were very upset, so in 1672 Henry was arrested and brought to London. After two pleasant years mingling with high society in London, he was knighted by King Charles II and sent back to Jamaica. He died in Jamaica in 1688 from over-indulging himself with food and drink. He was given a state funeral with a twenty-two gun salute.

Three daring and successful attacks by Captain Morgan

1) In 1668 he led an attack on Portobello, just along from Nombre de Dios, which Drake had attacked unsuccessfully years before. Portobello was now used as a port for shipping treasure out to Spain. Henry acted stealthily, landing five hundred men on the shore in darkness, using small rowing boats. The attack was made by land, which surprised the Spanish. The town was captured and its inhabitants held hostage until a ransom of 350,00 was paid by the president of Panama.

2) In 1669, when he attacked Maracaibo in Venezuela, Henry outwitted the Spanish admiral defending the port by disguising a merchant ship to look as if it had been customized by pirates with extra cannon and extra men. His men stuck logs through holes cut in the side of the ship, like cannons, and stood logs on the deck dressed in sailors' clothes. He also pretended that he was going to

attack from land, as he had in Portobello. He sent rowing boats filled with men to the shore. These were then rowed back to the ship with the men lying out of sight on the bottom of the boats.

3) In 1671 he attacked Panama with two thousand men of various nationalities, including English, French and Dutch, a fleet of thirty-nine ships and a commission from Jamaica appointing him admiral of the fleet. But the Spanish had already emptied most of the treasure from Panama and they blew up the city with gunpowder when they realized the buccaneers were going to capture it. Henry and the buccaneers took enough loot to load up 175 mules but when it was shared out between everyone who had taken part, there wasn't much to go round.

Buccaneers and their Books

The buccaneers were educated men. Many of them published books in London about their adventures at sea.

Lionel Wafer

Lionel Wafer was a buccaneer surgeon who was cared for by Indians in Panama when he was injured in 1681. When he came back to England, he wrote a book about his experiences.

Basil Ringrose

Basil Ringrose was a buccaneer surgeon. He wrote about the adventures of his fellow buccaneers in Panama, with detailed maps of the area.

William Dampier and Woodes Rogers

William and Woodes were buccaneers who sailed around the world together between 1708-1711. They picked up a man who had been marooned for four years on the desert island of Juan Fernandez, off the coast of Chile. William Dampier recognized the man as Alexander Selkirk, who had sailed with him years before. They took him on board ship as a crew member. When they got back to England, Woodes Rogers wrote an account of the voyage. (William Dampier had already written about his earlier adventures in two books.) The story of a man being marooned for four years was the basis for Daniel Defoe's story of Robinson Crusoe – about a man being marooned for twenty-five years.

CHAPTER NINE

Black Bart and the Pirates of the Caribbean

Daniel Defoe

The writer Daniel Defoe died in 1731, shortly after the Golden Age of Piracy came to an end. He lived in London and although he never left Britain, he loved stories about pirates that he heard in the taverns of Wapping. He used to go to prisons in London and interview people who had been sentenced to death and then write up their stories. He wrote a number of books, including *Robinson Crusoe*, about a man marooned on a desert island. He is also said to have published a book in 1724, under the name of Captain Johnson, called *A General History of the Robberies and Murders of the Most Notorious Pirates*. A great title, isn't it? Captain Johnson tells colourful stories about famous pirates who 'infested the waters' of the Caribbean.

Black Bart's Taste for Tea and Music

When Black Bart sailed from London in November 1719 as second mate on a merchant ship, he was still known as plain Bartholomew Roberts. In February 1720 his ship was captured by the pirate Captain Davies and Bart was forced to join them. He replaced Davies as captain and decided he preferred being a pirate captain to being an ordinary sailor.

Bart didn't like drinking alcohol, he preferred tea. Back home, gentlemen opted for coffee when they didn't want alcohol. Tea was considered a drink suitable for a lady.

He was very fond of music, even forcing two fiddlers to join his crew and play music on deck while he attacked other ships. He gave all his musicians the day off on Sunday.

Black Bart commanded five hundred men and a fleet of four ships, capturing four hundred prizes in his short career. Captain Skyrm was in charge of one of the ships in Bart's fleet and, even when he lost his leg in a battle, he carried on fighting. When all hope seemed lost, Skyrm's crew fired into the powder store to blow up the ship, rather than surrender.

Bart's motto was 'A merry life and a short one'. Two years after he became a pirate he was dead, killed in 1722 in an attack by a British warship. When he was killed, Bart's body was thrown overboard, as he had requested – so that it couldn't be displayed in chains.

Black Bart's Men and the Dutchman's Sausages

Blackbeard and his crew plundered the ship of a Dutch captain who was very upset when the pirates took some of his wife's homemade sausages, hung them round their necks and then threw them overboard, as if they weren't even fit to be eaten. Then the pirates killed the Dutch captain's chickens and invited him to dinner. The final insult was when they got drunk, picked up his prayer book and starting singing rude songs in French and Spanish, pretending they were reading from the Dutch words on the pages.

The Dutchman got his own back, though; while the pirates were off attacking another ship, he stole the gold they had hidden in their sea chests and escaped with it.

Edward Low and Other People's Ears

Edward Low was born in Westminster. He came from a family of criminals and used to bully other boys in the neighbourhood into giving him money, progressing to cheating while gambling with the footmen at the House of Commons. One of his brothers was a pickpocket and housebreaker who was hanged for stealing but another brother was a sailor who persuaded Edward (known as 'Ned') to go to sea with him, perhaps hoping to save him from a life of crime. It wasn't long before Ned turned to piracy in the

Spanish Main, running a black flag up the mast of a sloop and attacking other vessels.

Ned was accidentally wounded by a cutlass, which struck him on the chin. The cut was so deep that his teeth could be seen, and a surgeon was called to sew it up. Unfortunately he was drunk and when Ned criticized his handiwork, the surgeon told Ned to do it himself if he didn't like it, and punched him so hard that the stitches came out. You'd think the surgeon would be killed for his behaviour but there's no record that he was punished. The trouble was that there was only ever one surgeon on a ship so, unless they captured a ship and forced another surgeon to join them, they were stuck with the man they'd got.

In 1723 Ned Low, in the *Fancy*, gave chase to a Portuguese ship coming from Brazil. When his men went aboard, they couldn't find the treasure they were expecting. Eventually they discovered – by torturing some of the men – that during the chase, the captain had hung a bag containing 11,000 gold coins by a rope out of the window and when they were caught, he cut the rope so the bag fell into the sea, rather than give it up to the pirates. Ned was so angry that he cut off the Portuguese captain's lips and cooked them in front of him before killing him and all his crew.

Later that year, he cut off the ears of Captain Willard of

the Amsterdam Merchant, plundered his ship and then let him sail away.

He cut off the ears of Nathan Skiff, captain of a small whale-fishing boat, shot him and sunk his boat.

The next time he cut off the ears of the captain of a whaler, he made him eat his own ears. Ned supplied salt and pepper although there is no record of whether he cooked the ears first. The captain bravely swallowed them down without a murmur, although they must have been gristly and he must have been in considerable pain.

Ned also cut off the ears of a Captain Thompson and set fire to his new fourteen-gun ship, recently built in London to replace the *Rose*, which Ned had taken from Captain Thompson the year before.

When Ned had an argument with some of his men and wanted to punish them, he put pieces of wood between their fingers, set fire to the wood until the flesh on their fingers burned and melted away, attacked them with knives and cutlasses, then marooned them.

Copycat Captain Spriggs

Captain Spriggs sailed with Captain Low and later went off

on his own. He had a jolly roger made with exactly the same design as Ned Low's flag – a black background with a white skeleton plunging a dagger into a bleeding heart with one hand, and holding an hourglass in the other hand. You might think he had no imagination as he couldn't even think up an original design for his flag. But this obviously wasn't the case because when he captured a Captain Hawkins, Spriggs made him eat a plate of candles at gunpoint, then marooned him on a desert island.

Blackbeard

Blackbeard was married fourteen times, apparently without bothering to divorce, the last time in 1717 to a sixteen-year-old girl, even though he had a wife and children in London.

In 1718 a bounty was put on his head – £100 for him, £40 for any pirate captain captured near Virginia or North Carolina, dead or alive.

Once, when drunk, Blackbeard dared his men to go with him into the store where the powder was kept for their guns, close the hatches and set fire to several pots of powder, to see who could last in there the longest. The men coughed and spluttered and called out for him to open the hatches, so he was very pleased to have won (of course, perhaps they were humouring him 'cough, cough, ooh, please captain, you win'. Don't you think that otherwise he might have kept thinking up crazy, dangerous dares until he won one of them?) As Blackbeard explained, after he shot his first mate Israel Hands in the knee, maiming him for life, 'Unless you shoot one of your men from time to time, they forget who's boss.'

The night before he died, as he sat up drinking with his men, so the story goes, they asked him if his wife knew where his treasure was buried. 'No one knows except the Devil and me,' Blackbeard answered. Maybe it is still buried somewhere.

CHAPTER TEN

Pirate Lingo Bingo

Do you remember, at the beginning of the book, when you imagined travelling back in time to a tavern in Wapping to listen in to the pirates' stories? Wouldn't it be great if you could really do that? Then, if the pirates started telling a story about where to find some buried treasure, all you'd need to do is memorize the details, rush home and draw a map and then get some of your friends to go with you and help you dig it up.

There is one BIG PROBLEM. Pirates (and indeed all sailors) used so many specialized words and phrases that unless you had been to sea, it would have been very difficult to understand them. They talked about the mizzen (the mast at the back of the ship) or the poop (a short deck above the quarter deck, which was above the main deck) as if they were using a foreign language. And then, if that wasn't bad enough, they actually did use bits of foreign languages. My advice is that if you ever manage to invent a time machine, you should also work on something to translate any language in the world. In the meantime, let's play a game ...

There are lots of expressions in common use today that originated in nautical (sailing) terms. Most people don't know where these words or phrases originated from. This gives us the perfect chance to play Pirate Lingo Bingo!

Pirate Lingo Bingo

Bingo is traditionally a game for more than one player but I've adapted it so that you can play alone – see page 92. There are three ways to play – the listening version, the talking version and a play-along version:

1) The listening version

You will probably have heard these expressions before. They are used by people every day, even though they have no idea of their origin. Every time you hear one of these expressions – from your parents, teacher, grandparents or on television, if you watch it – put a tick in the box. When you've collected a full set of ticks Bingo! Congratulations.

2) The talking version – for extroverts only

Try and drop these expressions (in their current meaning) into your everyday conversations. Use as many as you can without anyone suspecting that you are playing a game. Give yourself a tick every time until you get the full set.

3) Play-along version – you need a friend for this

Make a list of five different expressions each. Decide whether you're going to be listening out for them or using them in your conversations. The first one to put a tick by all five expressions is the winner. How about buying a little bag of chocolate gold coins for a prize?

Here are the words and phrases:

Scuppered

Current meaning: Ruined, e.g. 'my plans have been scuppered'

The scuppers were the drains on deck and if a pirate fell or was knocked into the scuppers by a large wave he would have been injured or killed.

Touch and go

Current meaning: Uncertain, e.g. 'I hope she'll survive the accident but it's touch and go'

Pirates would have been referring to the fear of running aground – it was touch and go when a ship's keel touched bottom but then managed to go (get free).

At loggerheads

Current meaning: In disagreement, e.g. 'the union and the management are at loggerheads'

The loggerheads were two iron balls, one at each end of an iron bar, containing hot pitch for coating the wooden decks of a ship.

By and large

Current meaning: Pretty much, e.g. 'I think that by and large they agree with us'

To a pirate it would have meant sailing 'by' (with the wind) but 'large' (not close to the wind).

Between the devil and the deep blue sea

Current meaning: In a difficult position, e.g., 'I don't know whether to tell her she looks awful in that coat or let her go out like that. I'm between the devil and the deep blue sea'

In a pirate's time, the devil was the plank of wood going along the ship that was nearest the keel and therefore difficult (the devil) to get at when the ship was being coated in pitch to protect it from sea water. They might also have been talking about keel hauling, a punishment where men were tied to the keel (the devil) and dragged through the sea.

No room to swing a cat

Current meaning: Not much space, e.g., 'My bedroom is so small there's no room to swing a cat in here'

The cat was the cat o'nine tails, a kind of whip with thin pieces of leather or rope known as 'tails' on the end. It was used to 'flog' or beat sailors as a punishment.

The cat's out of the bag

Current meaning: The secret's out and there's going to be trouble, e.g. 'My sister told my auntie that my cousin is getting married so now the cat's out of the bag'

The cat o'nine tails was usually kept in a special red bag and was only removed to administer the punishment, so everyone knew that trouble was coming.

Chock-a-block

Current meaning: Crowded, e.g. 'I wish we'd left before

the rush hour, the roads are chock-a-block'

Sails were raised ('hoisted') using a piece of equipment (tackle) with two blocks on a rope and pulley system. The lower block moves up the rope until it touches the top one. When it was 'block-a-block' there was no more room for the sail to move up. This expression changed to 'chock-a-block'.

Get cracking

Current meaning: Get going quickly, e.g. 'The shops will be closed if we don't get cracking'

For the pirates, it meant adding more sails to make the ship go faster.

Third rate

Current meaning: Not very good, e.g. 'I don't want to play for some third-rate team, I want to win the cup'

A naval ship with 100 guns was classified first rate. A ship with 64-80 guns was classified third rate.

Lingo Bingo phrase	✓
Scuppered	
Touch and go	
At loggerheads	
By and large	
Between the devil and the deep blue sea	
No room to swing a cat	
The cat's out of the bag	
Chock–a–block	
Get cracking	
Third rate	

Lingo Bingo phrase	✓
Scuppered	
Touch and go	
At loggerheads	
By and large	
Between the devil and the deep blue sea	
No room to swing a cat	
The cat's out of the bag	
Chock–a–block	
Get cracking	
Third rate	

Other books from Watling St you'll love

CRYPTS, CAVES AND TUNNELS OF LONDON
By Ian Marchant
Peel away the layers under your feet and discover the
unseen treasures of London beneath the streets.
ISBN 1-904153-04-6

GRAVE-ROBBERS, CUT-THROATS AND POISONERS
OF LONDON
By Helen Smith
Dive into London's criminal past and meet some of its
thieves, murderers and villains.
ISBN 1-904153-00-3

DUNGEONS, GALLOWS AND SEVERED HEADS
OF LONDON
By Travis Elborough
For spine-chilling tortures and blood-curdling punishments,
not to mention the most revolting dungeons and prisons you
can imagine.
ISBN 1-904153-03-8

THE BLACK DEATH AND OTHER PLAGUES OF LONDON
By Natasha Narayan
Read about some of the most vile and rampant diseases ever
known and how Londoners overcame them – or not!
ISBN 1-904153-01-1

GHOSTS, GHOULS AND PHANTOMS OF LONDON
By Travis Elborough
Meet some of the victims of London's bloodthirsty
monarchs, murderers, plagues, fires and famines – who've
chosen to stick around!
ISBN 1-904153-02-X

RATS, BATS, FROGS AND BOGS OF LONDON
By Chris McLaren
Find out where you can find some of the creepiest and
crawliest inhabitants of London.
ISBN 1-904153-05-4

BLOODY KINGS AND KILLER QUEENS OF LONDON
By Natasha Narayan
Read about your favourite royal baddies and their
gruesome punishments.
ISBN 1-904153-16-X

HIGHWAYMEN, OUTLAWS AND BANDITS OF LONDON
By Travis Elborough
Take yourself back to the days when the streets of London
hummed with the hooves of highwaymen's horses and the
melodic sound of 'Stand and deliver!'
ISBN 1-904153-13-5

WITCHES, WIZARDS AND WARLOCKS OF LONDON
By Natasha Narayan
Quite simply the bizarre history of London, full of
superstition, magic and plain madness.
ISBN 1-904153-12-7

REBELS, TRAITORS AND TURNCOATS OF LONDON
By Travis Elborough
What could you expect if you were a traitor – and you were
discovered? Take your pick from some of the most
hideous punishments ever invented.
ISBN 1-904153-15-1

SPIES, SECRET AGENTS AND SPOOKS OF LONDON
By Natasha Narayan
Look through the spy hole at some of our greatest
spies and their exploits, to how to
make your own invisible ink.
ISBN 1-904153-14-3

In case you have difficulty finding any Watling St books in your local bookshop, you can place orders directly through

BOOKPOST
Freepost
PO Box 29
Douglas
Isle of Man
IM99 1BQ

Telephone: 01624 836000

email: bookshop@enterprise.net